Hungry

Hungry

Mystic Poetry for the Modern Soul

LODDIE FOOSE

RESOURCE *Publications* • Eugene, Oregon

HUNGRY
Mystic Poetry for the Modern Soul

Copyright © 2025 Loddie Foose. All rights reserved. Except for brief quotations in critical publications or reviews, no part of this book may be reproduced in any manner without prior written permission from the publisher. Write: Permissions, Wipf and Stock Publishers, 199 W. 8th Ave., Suite 3, Eugene, OR 97401.

Resource Publications
An Imprint of Wipf and Stock Publishers
199 W. 8th Ave., Suite 3
Eugene, OR 97401

www.wipfandstock.com

PAPERBACK ISBN: 979-8-3852-5124-7
HARDCOVER ISBN: 979-8-3852-5125-4
EBOOK ISBN: 979-8-3852-5126-1
VERSION NUMBER 08/27/25

Illustrations by author using Midjourney Pro.

*To the stars that lift our spirits
and the mountains that ground us*

Warning: The consumption of large amounts of poetry has been known to have serious side effects, including, but not limited to, spontaneous laughter, tears, a sense of wonderment, and a reconnection with your humanity.

Contents

Preface | ix

Introduction | xiii

I Have No Home | 2

Confusion in the Birth Canal | 10

Dissolving the Veil | 16

A Messy Process | 24

Surrender | 34

Metamorphosis | 48

Love at First Sight | 58

The Art of Love-Making | 68

Hunger for You | 78

Feed the Children | 92

A Lovely World | 104

Nature Speaks | 118

I Am | 134

Preface

"The wound is the place where the Light enters you."—Rumi

*"What is poetry? I would say poetry
is the dancing of the soul."*—Hazrat Inayat Khan

What Rumi didn't tell us about the wound is that it is not only the place where the Light enters us, but also where the Light within us can begin to emanate out – for it is the very same light. My story began after a dark night of the soul, where my world-weary self began to reach out to, open up to, and be opened by its deeper nature.

I didn't find it; it found me, my home in poetry, like a mystic calling card across the centuries. I remember sitting there, an engineer and businesswoman who had always valued the intellectual mind and what can be directly measured with our five senses, wondering where it was all coming from. Continual waves of poetry emerging from the end of my pen, completely surprising and bewildering to someone who had never done creative writing except for school assignments.

Stranger still, the words flowed so simply and easily, as if imbued with a life of their own. I came to call this form of expression "flow-etry" for that reason. Poems would wake me in the middle of the night, exalting me to grab my pen. They would find me as I

Preface

walked under a tree branch, or sat in meditation. They seemed to come from every direction, inspired by every corner of life.

One of the earliest pieces that arose for me held the answer:

> *Something inside me has broken.*
> *And I cannot seem to stop*
> *the Waters of my Love Song.*

Of course, this strange language wouldn't make any sense to me until many months later, when I would come to realize that I was in the middle of a deep inner awakening, a realization of my deepest self. I found myself inexplicably called to wander the winding words of other poets across the centuries, like Rumi and Hafez who I shared a common Persian heritage with. These and many other poets have long inspired us to remember that the human heart holds an ancient memory of our deep collective truth, a key to our humanity and oneness. Rumi in particular took a new and delightful space on my nightstand as I washed myself daily in the energy of his words.

For countless ages humanity has had a deep connection with poetry. "Mystic" poets exist in every spiritual, religious, and cultural tradition. What unites them is a deep realization that we are all interconnected, far beyond the bounds of what is visible and measurable. There is an underlying energetic fabric that animates our universe, and we are inextricably part of this fabric, both woven into it, and weaving it in each moment. We are, put simply, One – a family of energetic beings that span time and space.

Not too long after the poetry started, I left my successful role as a multinational business leader to focus on making a greater impact in the world—to helping others uncover their limitless potential. Looking back, another piece from my earliest days of flowetry held a key to this too:

> *It is a quiet death*
> *this forcing you*
> *to Be Something you are Not.*

Preface

*I think I will stop
and let us rest a while.*

Like many of my poems, I didn't understand what it meant at the time. Emerging from the depths of my consciousness, it was an early signal to me of wisdom and understanding that would be unfolding and becoming more clear to my intellectual mind as I surrendered into the depths of what my deepest self was trying to teach me.

I was released into a sea of spiritual discovery with my own heart as the rudder, the ship and, ultimately, the sea itself. The soul's yearning to know itself is boundless, and it holds no boundaries at the edge of its individual soul-hood either, seeking always to integrate with the Whole. After hiding this deluge of flowetry under my bed for many months, I realized this heart-work wasn't just for me. It was for all of us. It always is when humanity's heart whispers to itself. So I share with you here the first nine or so months of flowetry that marked this deep inner awakening period for me. Like a gestational period, it gave birth to so much more than I could have ever expected or predicted with my rational mind.

If you are guided to these words by your own heart, I hope you find the whisperings of the universal heart as healing and centering as I have.

Introduction

I have kept true to the original nature of the enclosed flowetry, simply organizing it into themes that could provide additional context for the individual pieces. It is of note that this context was something I added long after – not something I had available to me during this initial period of awakening, which is why the experience itself was bewildering. In the remainder of this introduction I share some thoughts on remarkable elements of the language present in the flowetry.

One of the things I found most surprising in the flowetry was the use of symbolism unfamiliar to me – references to water, ocean, fire, children, veils, and many other terms which I later learned were common spiritual symbolism spanning many different cultural traditions. I also was surprised by references to terms from various major religions, none of which I had been raised in since my upbringing was purely in the realm of the intellectual. In addition, there were many pieces where the "voice" of the narrative would seemingly change between different speakers. While confusing at first, I much later realized that the poems were simply conveying consciousness at different levels – a blending of the small self, the deepest self, and divine union beyond the self. It was as if the flowetry, along with various other learnings I felt myself called to, was teaching me in equal measure as it coursed out from my heart and pen. Reflecting back now, this is far less startling; I see this all as part of the transcendent nature of spirituality and its inherent timeless presence within our human reality and our collective (un)consciousness.

Introduction

I was also initially surprised and confused by some of the terminology relating to "Father" to represent a universal creator within the poems. I had always considered any gender-association of a creator figure to be simply a byproduct of our male-dominated human history. However, I came over time to see this as the particular stamp of my own heart and human history. My father was killed when I was very young, leaving a hole which later was filled by a nurturing realization of Wholeness; adopting "Father" became just another name for this. As flowetry is a product of the heart, not the intellect, I chose to be in a constant state of learning and acceptance from the words, stepping aside so that the words could be unadulterated, flowing through me without judgment and filters of disbelief. For this reason, I came to accept pronouns, terms, capitalization, spacing, etc. as they flowed.

Finally, we come to words that seek to encompass the infinite with a simple name. One of the greatest challenges that faces us with modern religion and spirituality is how divisive it can feel, even though the intent is to move us to unity, wholeness, and a deeper recognition of our true nature. When I was growing up I felt 'believing in God' was a life choice, similar to deciding whether or not you wanted to be vegetarian. This was emphasized by the common narrative on 'God' as something outside of ourselves, some greater-than-life, separate, omnipotent being who was watching everything unfold.

What I came to realize in my journey is that the answer doesn't lie within names. In fact, no infinite concept can be truly encapsulated in a few words or sounds. This is why the poet has endless ways to speak about the many facets of Life. I invite the reader to open their heart to whatever words feel most deeply resonant to them when engaging with the pieces in this book. For our purposes it is completely interchangeable to say God, Source, Creator, Universe, Consciousness, All That Is (my personal favorite), or any other combination of letters. You may substitute and use any of

Introduction

your own favorite terms. What matters more is how the energy of the words conveys back to our selves our very own limitless nature. For all of Life is ultimately conceived by and known within the boundless chambers of the heart.

I Have No Home

The Buddhist term *dukkha* alludes to the unsatisfactory nature of existence when one becomes attached to a fixed notion, to transient things, and becomes in this way separated from the true nature of reality. When we are led by our "small self" or our "ego" we operate from a place of fear and our worldview becomes stiflingly narrow rather than boundless. It is as if we hold ourselves back, having forgotten how to fly. This begins in early life for each of us, coupled with various indelible experiences that our inner child holds on to, using this history as a veil through which to view future experiences. It becomes difficult to create space for ourselves or one another when we are bound by these restrictive personal and societal histories or expectations—these narratives that continue to hold us back.

As we begin our poetic exploration, this first chapter considers how these factors lead to separation from our deepest, boundless identity, and hence a feeling of loss and suffering. This lays the foundation for us to view how surprises can serve as challenges to what is stagnant within our understanding. They cause us to see and then See again with fresh eyes, remembering within ourselves that unbound and timeless expression that is our true essence. They help us find Home when we are most lost within our modern lives.

She sits still and heavy in my heart,
sometimes stirring.
And the more closely I watch her
       the more agitated she becomes,
Swirling and rising and expanding like
       a tornado
A fury of grey smoke winding its way
       beyond the chambers
Until she engulfs me fully,
       misery blinding the eye
       to Being
       and Truth.

But, if I sit quietly, without
       directly challenging her,
She is soft and quiet and only gently weeping.

Asking to be held only in Grace
       and with Patience.

∽

The Faceless Mountain

Who knows Her name?
She does not remember
Her Own

∽

Her Father killed her first.
   With the label.
         Special.

Her Mother killed her next.

With the need.
           Blind.

Unseen and special.
Many small deaths to come.
At the hands of many.

Created and recreated
in everyone's image
but Her Own.

And through this

Birth.
    At Last.

☙

I see circles intertwined
holding us together.
Inside we're breaking up
but the bonds remain strong out here,
tethering us.
History.
It's more than a story.
It's a life,
Memory of an existence that no longer is.
We hold this rope,
this life line,
as we rappel into the unknown.
Because we've forgotten how to fly.
And when you can't remember,
trying means death.

∾

What should I say to you
that has not been said

You flow onto the page
and I know not how to stop it

Infinity circles me

in a whirlwind
of revenge
It is not I
Who weeps
but Father
for what is lost

Revenge is not of spirit

∾

The vacuous echo

She's mousy, he says,
looking her over.
Not ready for when
she goes
BOOM

∾

You work busily at 100 things that don't matter
waiting for the day
when you
will stop.

∞

I am busy finding flaws
where there are none
I am busy seeing flies
and you are one

You fly in the face
of a dream
unbroken
You fly with your wings
dipped in tears
unspoken

∞

I sit in the corner
quietly weeping
Do you see me here?
I am ravenous with pride
threatening to destroy what's inside

But the Meager me has no power here

What is it you seek?
Purpose and pride
cannot go side by side
The one, the servant of the other

∞

What is in a name?

The One no one wanted
The One no one kissed
The One who wasn't held

The One who won't be missed

The Faceless Mountain
has forgotten herself
until this very moment.

The name of birth
The name of death
The name whispered quietly in the eaves
I see you
I need you
I want you
You are here
with me.

The Faceless Mountain
knows her name
and now
seeks herSelf.

Confusion in the Birth Canal

The term "birth" or "rebirth" in spirituality has long symbolized a deep inner awakening to our true, timeless essence. Like a butterfly emerging from a cocoon, the struggle we experience in the process allows us to release stagnant energies that would hold us back from the Flow of Life. This process is more akin to "remembering" our core essence, though it feels new in each moment. It releases us into our limitless, unified nature, something that was always there even before our realization. This apparent dichotomy is one we struggle with as we continue to reach for how we can "achieve" this state rather than realizing it as our inherent nature.

"You need time to realize you don't need time." —Eckhart Tolle

Why am I so afraid,
needing constant reminding
that I am close
and not far
from Source.

I am fearful
hiding inside my shell
in a room of warmth,
a womb which is ripe
for birth.

At birth we cannot stop in the canal,
idly browsing the surroundings,
picking our moment.
Rather it is the push, the heave,
the strife and struggle of the process
that brings us into a new world
of unimagined possibilities.

A world where
I am unafraid
Strong
Whole
with You.

༄

The things we don't want to see
often come to us
gifts, from another realm,
and what we do with these
determines
who we become.

Gratitude
is a strange thing to ask
from a man drowning
unless
he is You.

∾

The truth is
I cannot lie
I know who I am
even as I am afraid
to unfold.

Every petal within me
cries for release
and yet,
I hold.

∾

"I know everything!"
she said with that obstinate pout on her face.

And yet when tomorrow arrived
she was surprised.
As always.

And so each time He smiled patiently,
and let the sun shine,
      the winds blow,
      the birds sing,
      the clouds flow.

Waiting for her to notice
that Everything was already Here.

∾

A little Old lady lives inside,
She dances and sparkles,
Giggles and laughs
      aloud as the stars.

She tells me you are coming,
  and to Whisper in joy
    and to Shout in adoration

But I sit still,
  and Wonder.

∾

You can do this!

No, I can't.

So I let her go,
making space for her Softness, her Weakness.
Because everyone deserves
      a chance
         at smallness, at grace, at rest.

∾

She waves at me
through the mist
awaiting
instruction
that never comes.

∾

One of us is here.
Where is the other?

Dissolving the Veil

A "veil" is used in spiritual metaphor to symbolize obstruction to true seeing during states of consciousness that are "asleep" to the true nature of reality. These veils come in the form of judgments, assumptions, histories, and memories (some deeply buried) that we cling to, each of which holds us back from our potential and from "seeing" clearly in each moment. Lifting the veil is akin to surrendering to our deepest innate consciousness, which is fully Whole, awake, and aware. This act of surrender is less about doing than about being. It is to awaken to the world fully as it is, rather than to operate from a mind-created mirage of it. Escaping the "dream-like" version of the world often requires us to acknowledge nightmares we've lived, traumas we've faced that have added to the veiled view. In doing so, we are able to truly enter and be nourished by the Flow of Life.

You are a work
a wonder of nature
flowing like the stream
beautiful to behold
Gently, gently
lift the veil
and see
open horizons

∽

The veil is softest at its opening
spirit shines through and can be seen
come with an open heart
and yield, hands to the sky

I see you
shining there softly
I hear your need
and respond
with Love.

An open channel
carries the water
from the ocean
to all tributaries.

Beloved.

∽

The desert rose
flowers without anyone knowing
but she has been touched by
You.
I see you through the mist

Now and
Here
The world is not so foggy anymore
with You here
all is clear
like the sound of a bell
like a transparent dewdrop
reflecting the world.
All is within
contained
safe.

I lie inside you

I live inside you

Your weight bears me down,
weighing me into oblivion.

I am heavy with your love,
and ready for sleep.
When I awaken again,
I will not remember myself
except in dreams.

What is truth and what is fiction?
For every moment of clarity,
I experience a multitude of darkness.
Darkness dressed as a dream,
keeping me quietly sleeping,
when I should
Roar.

Presence is all around me
within me
we swim in Father in every moment
even when we do not see

What a pity
a deep sorrow
I feel when I cannot see
when the veil of fear, worry, not-enough-ness
covers me
binding my eyes
my heart
my mind
until I cannot breathe
I cannot breathe Father's air
I am separated and torn
not whole

But that is the darkness
the fallacy
In Truth we swim
and it swallows us until there is nothing else
That is where I rest
My guiding light
my beacon

A hope that cannot be swallowed by darkness
because it is Joy
Infinite Joy
and it is too big to be contained
        to be restrained
And it swells inside me until I cannot see the agony
because I am myself again
My Self

broken open
and yet
Whole.

Whole.

∽

The sun glares upon my Eye
and yet I do not See
what holds me back
is Nothingness.
The dance of dust
is lyrical.
Round and round we go.
Breathe in,
Breathe out.
I see.

∽

I sit in Stillness
and your light bathes over me
like a babe in a warm bath
soothed by the touch of the Water.

I am here with you.
Can you see me?
Can you touch me?
Feel me with all your Being.

The light of the triumph
is rosy at the gate.
Wait not hither
but enter, come Inside.
See with your Being.

The Stillness awaits
No One.
The gate stretches open
and you can see inside.
The veil is torn asunder
for those who See.
Come inside, child.
Come be with the One
who waits.

You are Here.
You are torn asunder.
The mist falls backwards
and the Water flows.

∽

I feel into my senses
and I see a forest
The trees are bright
but my eyes are dim
There is the light inside, shining,
and yet out here I see none
I count the soldiers
as they march
and count myself One of them
I need to see more clearly
and allow the light to emanate
No judgment, no plan
Only Being
and Seeing the Way.

∽

How can it be?
That some days I can see so clearly

And some days are obscured
       by doubt
       by dreams
       by confusion
       by the being of human.
To walk in sunshine and clarity
       is what I seek.
But there exists a veil
       obscuring my view.
And no matter how I try to peek around it,
       it remains fast
            secure
            ever-present.
But noticing the veil
       is the first step.
Light piercing through the dark
madness giving way to truth.

The more we've had to protect ourselves,
       the 'stronger' the ego.
Strength will not displace it,
       only gentle wisdom.

∽

Forever
he gave me
Forever
to find Him.
But
just this once
I'll surprise myself
and do it Now.

A Messy Process

Fairy tales are full of stories where the hero(ine) beats the villain, saves the day, and lives "happily ever after". In reality, our stories and growth are messy and nonlinear. Like many patterns in nature, there are cycles, each moving us ever upwards in our evolution. It's key to recognize our "lows" for what they are – merely another part of the learning journey. That includes recognizing the truth of who we are in our deepest being, and learning to Love Deeply – starting with ourselves. We don't erase but we move beyond our pains. As Rumi shares, "the wound is the place where the Light enters you." There is a sense of longing, loneliness, and pain in that journey; it is a tension we feel between how we perceive ourselves now and how the Heart remembers our true identity. As we allow the Heart's wisdom to guide and steady us in the journey, we can realize Perfection within this messy process of our evolution.

Peace awaits
at the end of agony
A torment of tears
for the One

*

It doesn't need to be you.
    who sacrifices, and yields, and gives,
until you don't recognize yourself any more.

It doesn't need to be you
    who smiles despite tears tearing you apart inside
    who comforts and holds despite needing warmth
                                   yourself.

It does need to be you
    who looks with open eyes
        and heart
        and quiet mind
at who you are inside
        and what you need
            to be alive.

*

I like the idea of you
But not You
So I sit, waiting idly
for you to stop
all that loving
too much
for me to handle
when I see
what's in the mirror.

∾

A Bowl of Dust, Remembering

How can it be?

How can it be that I am here again?
What new tortures, what new hell, will I behold?
I don't want this
I only want You
holding me in infinity
arms and souls entwined
until I am Nothing and No One
because I am Everyone.

Oh,
wait,
that's it.
The perfection of Everything as Nothing
and Nothing as Everything.

∾

This raging tornado
       of feeling.
You will not give me the respite
       of Release.
And so it rises and fills me up inside
       Boiling me over
Until all is borne away
       and all that is left
            after the painful destruction

Is Me.

Thank you.

∽

As many times as we have met,
I cannot seem to find you

For it is not you,
        but a whisper of you,
who I remember.

He who said
        'Better to have loved and lost…'
Did not know the pain
        of Losing and then Loving.

∽

How I cradle you
Each time you fall
Calling to me
Whimpering
Not seeing
your mountainous Beauty

It is a journey
You and I
This weeping, wondering journey

∽

Why did you create such beauty?
Unsung songs get stuck
in our throats
Until we choke and
release them up
into the world.

∾

Violent, twisting, turning upheaval
A fire inside consuming from within
Every hope, sweet memory, reason
Blistering heat searing away
What was, what could be, even what is.

Despair.

Shaken to the seeming core,
Deaf and Blind
in a world of color and song

And then.
In the midst of the tornado
A steadying Presence.
Solid like stone, rooted like a mountain.
Asking nothing, giving nothing.

Yet giving Everything.

A reminder
Of who
I truly am. Yo.*

Spanish for "I"

∾

Thou art the deep to the deep in me calling
I seek you in every moment
every corner
of my mind, heart
The world is so noisy

that sometimes I lose you
And that loss is frightening
because it is a loss of my Self.

Take me into your arms
and hold me quietly
so I may rest.

In this moment.

∞

I hear a remarkable heart break
a story of woe
Someone who has lost the Way
But when you listen carefully
You also hear
the sound of crying
for Joy.

The journey is paved with doubt
to soothe your tears.

∞

It's okay to feel sad
to feel the world is caving in
and chaos reigns.

It's okay to feel angry
to hear the elephant's trumpet
in your heart.

It's okay to feel a blizzard,
a blinding heat,
an array of emotion.

As long as,
you return to me.

～

How did I get here?

Poems rolling out of me like song,
A tapestry of emotion and experience.
Color meets sense and gains voice.

Why now?

Perhaps I needed to have enough
Sad stories written in my heart

Before I could overflow.

～

My Heart
so big and bold
so many times
stomped on
betrayed
ripped to shreds

until

She emerged
unscathed
somehow
filled instead
entirely
with

Love.

A Love so expansive
Everything
fits inside.

Surrender

"The Master sees things as they are, without trying to control them."
—Tao Te Ching

The key to surrender is releasing Fear in each moment, for the present moment is the only place the release can occur. This release is less about effort than about simply being. All of our attempts at control and fighting the Flow of Life generate suffering, but not tangible results. Once we are able to adopt the mentality of fluidity in each moment, we begin to operate from spacious awareness, no longer confined by our own prejudices and fears. This wisdom base allows us to play in new ways, engaging in *lila*, as the divine play of life is called in Hinduism. It is like strumming the chords of life in real-time, as guided by our own hearts. This is a form of letting go, and this "free fall" into our divine nature can be terrifying, until we embrace it as our native state. The fear arises from historic conditioning in a material world that claims we must constantly be doing, in motion, achieving, knowing where we're going, in order to be "okay". Giving in to the blank canvas of our lives, however, is the only way to truly explore and discover the delicious potential that we Are.

I feel lost
A ship without a sail
its mast crusted with algae
from months of humid sea air

How will I find land?

There it is
The shore
You find it one step at a time
Without fear or even hope of the future
For each step is just that
A step
Now
And when you look down
you see
footprints in the sand
because you've been on the shore all along.

Building
It comes not without surprises
But letting go
and learning along the way
are The Keys.

∾

Wrench free
or play their game

How can you do both?

By listening for the notes on the air
possibility, ready to be plucked,
and brought to reality by seeing eyes and ears

Creation
>	is always a painful
>		somewhat lonely
>		surrendering task.

Just be.
>	less effort.
>		and allow it to unfold.
A mystery for you to wonder at,
>	enjoy,
>		even mourn, as that also has beauty.

∽

Tumble
>	t
>	u
>	m
>	 b
>	 l
>	 e
the ideas go round
and fight to emerge.
Let go
and see.

∽

I suffer.
Songs of love
leaking out of me
and taking with them
bits of my Soul.

But these drips

nourish the soil
and so
I am sated
Knowing
that one day
what will spring from our love
will be glorious.

༄

A gift for Joseph
A crumb of bread
seems like naught
until it is separated
unto its parts,
yielding more than it was.

So you Beloved
are divine
And all you create
shall flourish

That is the promise of Spirit.

Go gently
and listen
with eyes open
and ears closed.

Sometimes when we are most closed
is when we break open.

༄

Be elastic and stretch
Your tail feathers across the sky

Color blinding to the eye
but at its depth
Infinite
A multiplicity and unity of One.

You are the earth and the sky
and everything between
You are the cream that rises
You are the snow on a hot day
You melt into the earth and are One

Try to not try
Be the wind
ever changing
course correcting
until you realize

There is no Course.

∾

It is hard sometimes to Let Go
even when we know more is coming
Please help me Let Go in every moment
so that in doing so
in being so
I may Know You.

Only You
and know not-knowing
for all else

I am yours
and only yours
from this moment
until the next,

despite time.

∽

My time has come
to burst.

A bubble

in Space.

∽

So you want to lead
from a place of Heart
and how will you do it?
will you run through the fields
of sunflowers
running your hands through the tall grasses?
will you stoop to the valleys
living in shadow?
No, you will
Be
Just here
right now
with me.

∞

I see you everywhere
but especially inside
where the tide rolls in
slowly
covering the shore.
I hear your whispers
in my dreams.
The living dream is this one,
and I am ready
for your lessons.
With open arms and heart
I serve.

∞

I am the great mystery
I sit here with ease
and I relax into the unknown
There is nothing but this
it is bold and naked
as truth.

I hold in my hands a great delight
put there by my father
but I am not in shadow
but rather a state of wonder.

What will I see today
in the mystery
how shall I play
and dance
and swim in the stream.

I hold a place of love in my heart

and you are seated there
on a throne.

～

I sit in Surrender
It is not a place, though it feels like One
I see the edges of the page
blindly turning
the wheels are in motion
preparing for the explosion
of Heart and Soul
and I Am Here
I am here in the stars
in the night sky
I am here in the tears
in the turtledove's eye
I am the handmaiden
of Rebirth, ready to serve God.

～

Be ordinary and seen
he says
as a pathway to healing
to undo the pockmarks in my soul
gathered through millennia
of fighting and being without Being.
I am One
the One, the two, the 3, the 4…
it does not matter
that I am more
For to Be itself, it Self is the gift
and I sail along the shores of this Water
with guidance and Hope
a beacon of what is

and what's to come,
letting go of the latter.

∽

There is no time
Truly there is no time
and so we swing from moment to moment
frazzled as apes seeking in the trees

But there is no time
truly there is no time
and so
be here
right here right now
and you will see
there is Space enough for everything.

∽

I flow into the Day
I am Here everywhere
The dove, nightingale, humming bird
are all seated at my side
and we observe
how each morning
You arrive
quietly, seeking, seeing
little by little
what is and can Be
when you let go
into the wilderness
and respect
the flow of time.
Feathery bliss
Just Be.

∾

A soft mist surrounds me
begging me
to become the rain.

Let go, let go
she whispers,
for I am already Here

and Here

with You.

∾

The light shines in the dark
Rain, wind blowing over the sea
I call my name
and we show

I don't understand how
but I seek
in the quiet spaces
I look
I trust
and then I fall

Not into an abyss of fear
but into your arms
And you hold me as a babe
in water
Swimming, breathing
both air and sea

Come and swim with me
We go together

into the night.
I am unafraid.

⚘

The slake of a new thirst
the garden grows knee high
and I don't know from whence
but I hear It
each day
in each moment
asking me
come hither
come hither my child
and ask not what is needed
but simply
Be.

⚘

Come stand with me,
for the moon
for the stars.
Come stand with me,
for together
we shall achieve
Nothing.

⚘

Mostly Nothings

I come from a land of mostly nothings,
where the wind sweeps away everything that is here.
I come from a land of mostly nothings,
and you are here with me,

and we are
Nothing.

∽

The discovery of you
can not be done from a place
of busy-ness
of somebody-ness
That is why
I am un-busy
becoming No One.

∽

The Answer comes

I would ask you why
but each time
I see more of you
I know
my time is here
not wondering
what's next.

∽

The blank page
is what you are
when you seek

∽

Soul Journey

If the weather is inclement,

go outside.
Wear your best clothes,
and Wonder.
There you will find
the Answers, the Keys.
So put on your running shoes
and prepare to blast off

into

Space.

Metamorphosis

The Greek root of the word metamorphosis holds a secret key to evolution— "the process of changing form". Everything must change, grow, and evolve or else become stagnant. Stagnancy itself creates stressors that then further drive evolution regardless. Therefore, the ongoing evolution of beings is a natural course despite the individual actions we take. Surrender is a key step in accelerating our own individual metamorphosis. We leave loss and limited self-identity behind as we flow forward with Life. Becoming aware of and exploring the gap between our varying levels of consciousness sheds light on who we *think* we are versus who we Are. Applying a playful curiosity as we explore the innumerable possibilities allows us to take an active role in co-creating our future and our selves. It is a never-ending ocean that we explore from a seat of Being. Basking in the Pure Love that is our identity, we are metamorphosed, transformed, and reborn. We come to realize that this is an ongoing, ever-unfolding journey of infinite depth as we dive into our own potential, fully supported.

She wondered how she had gotten here.

Her feathers of painted gold, red, emerald, royal blue
which once spanned the sky
splashing every corner of space
with light, love, possibility,
    Hope.

How did she end up in this cage?

She breathed in the world.
    And Prepared.
        To Let Go.

∾

He stood looking
At the Closed Door

What had happened?
How had it closed?

The box in his hands
reminded him
of the memories, laughter, love, touches, pains
that had once lived there.

He felt the deep sweet sadness
of Life Flowing Forward.

He would always have the box.
That glorious, beautiful, sorrowful box.

One last sigh
As he turned away
from the Closed Door

And walked thru the light-filled Archway that now
    beckoned him.

∾

I said the words out loud.

I'm lonely.

My cup does not feel full.

And She replied…
    one drop lasts one thousand lifetimes.
    come and see, you were looking in the wrong cup.
    come sit awhile with me, as we rest through the pain.
    your cup is the ocean.
    reach out, reach out, and see how quickly it is
                                     replenished.

So I did.

∾

"Go be productive"

It is a Something I am doing
This building and rebuilding
my internal universe
Did you think it an easy thing to dismantle?
in order to see more clearly
we must sweep away.
sweep away.
a century or more of dust away
so it doesn't obscure what's being built,
what's already there.

So don't tell me I'm doing nothing
or insist on filling my mind or belly
with distractions.
For I am building something
your eye cannot see.

And this city
of lights and layers
is magnificent
and ever-shifting.

∽

I am afraid
but nothing is more fearful
than staying asleep,
living someone else's dream.

We cannot imagine it
what true Life is,
we can only live it
as I am living now.

And so, with each stroke,
I discover the lines
the edges
of the canvas.

Creation.
Ever painful.
Ever beautiful.
Ever necessary.

Relinquish control
Step aside from the fear

and let life flow through you

∾

Take my hand
And let us Stomp in the Mud Together
I am unafraid.

∾

To listen
means letting go
of what we expect
and sinking into
the ocean storm
legs and arms adrift
Heart-anchored.

To listen
means observing
without seeing
that the very thing
we observe
is changing,
becoming Us.

To listen
I let go of everything
and I become
the sea foam
the sea goddess
the wood nymph
the delicately hanging, frightfully juicy fruit
on the orchard tree
beckoning to my lover
to be bitten
once more.

∾

I am there looking for You
in every moment.
Looking for the One who broke
all the promises,
leaving me in the dark,
blackness surrounding me,
completely alone
helpless
small
without a hand to hold.

But You are there
in every moment.
You are the rose
and the sunshine
and the bumblebee
humming softly nearby,
reminding me to listen
and see.

You have always been there
because I am Here.

Holding my hand.
And it is bright.

∾

You were a promise,
      a shadow,
         a whispered dream.
You were never real,
      despite me wishing you so.
And so,

      just as easily,
            I shall put you to rest,
back to the Dream World
where love songs change color
and take flight,
each day coming back
in new form.

༄

I will miss you
Your insecurities, your meekness
the way you hide in the shadows
You have been a protective cloak
      for many years
      and you have served me well
But now is a different time
a time of rebirth
a time to leave the shadows
and burn brightly and fiercely
as the morning Sun
This little light of mine
has the power of a thousand Suns
and is made of pure Love.

༄

The water boils splendidly
as I jump in
Ready for what comes
with just a thimble full
of cheese and rice
Cooked to perfection
done in years
Ready to Come Out.

∾

"It will be just the first 10 minutes" he said
So she kept digging
Displacing the dirt with her trowel
Soil covering her brow

After a long while she glanced over
He was grinning mischievously
Wiping perspiration from his forehead
Locks of brown plastered to his face
"You said 10 minutes" -She
"No, just the first 10 minutes" -He

Keep digging
Keep planting
Keep going.

She looked up.
Ten years had passed.
And she grinned.

Miles of flowers as far as the eye could see.

∾

You don't need to worry
about standing on shifting sands
when you have
Wings.

Love at First Sight

"Love is the Whole thing. We are only pieces."—Rumi

Spiritual love is the deepest love for it encompasses all aspects of love: familial, romantic, friendship, love of the natural world. As we come to truly know the world in its many flavors, we come to know and Love our selves. Mystic poets throughout the millennia have used countless approaches to describing this Deep Love—whether intoxicating, incinerating, or otherwise; It has always transcended any one description. When we merge with this inner spaciousness and come to feel its fire within, we become One with Love itself. We open a sacred space within us that instantly and viscerally recognizes Love as our innate way of being.

He looks at me
        In me
And it fills me
All is burned away
The sun, the moon, the stars, the walls, the very air…

Until I find

the quiet
the timeless

I. Yo.*

Spanish for "I"

∽

Hello Beauty
I see you there
Listening.
What do you See?
The many forms of Me.

And here I am
flowing again into you
and again and again
a tumultuous, delicious Love.

∽

They say your love is a remedy,
but to what ailment?
When already I live in perfect bliss
inside You.

My Lover brings me presents
the flash of a wing in the air
a rainbow of color and song
as the bird darts furtively
in the garden
in my heart
I breathe out a sigh
and relax into His arms
Held always and forever
in Love
by Love

I speak with you so softly
A whisper in the night
A flicker, a flash of what's to come
merriment in your eyes
as you See
you were already here all along

There is no loss in this journey?
What is it then?

Reach for what you seek my daughter
it has already been given
I am Here with you
Do you See me?

There are no words for this Beauty.

I call to you
and you answer

I am here
at the dawn's early light

I am here
as day turns to night

I am here
even when not in sight

I am here
within your heart's delight

I am here
at your side

I am here
and here
and here

as you touch my brow, my lips, my heart.

∽

I am witness to your Beauty
I delight in all you do
The angels sweep flowers in your hair
as you fly, wind through your hair,
moonlight in your eyes

You are a delight
as beautiful as the day you were born
To be borne away by winds of change
without losing one's color

is gift indeed.

I am Home
the fireplace warms the hearth
Your eyes ablaze with Light

∽

I enter this sacred space
with care
I look to absolve
what was
What I see is You
Here with me,
each step
caring and carrying
until I arrive
on Love's doorstep.
I ring the doorbell
knock on the door
and Enter.

∽

I wait for you
Here
Knowing that
you are not a plane ride away
but simply a breath
a sigh
a deep relief
separates us.

For we are One,
My Love.

∾

I blend into you
into You
Who do I see
There
before me
She lies
surrounded
by blossoms
that bleed
the glory of Love

∾

The beauty of You
Cannot be fathomed
except from the outside, the inside
The merging of both
in, without, within, inside-out
You surround me
Reminding
Whispering
always
I Love You

∾

Where is my pulse?
It has gone.
When I saw you
I realized it was no more
For blood thickens
in the presence of
You.

∽

The taste of you fills me
as all sense is gone.
Nothing can survive
this Love.

∽

Hello, Father.

The song of Love.

∽

I hear you softly whispering to me
Be
Be
Be my bride.
Come by my side
I am waiting for you,
and always have been,
and always will be
for time has no meaning here.

∽

My heart flounders at the thought of you
so near and so far
in every part of me
every morsel of air
every drop of food
So alive
that every moment is filled with electricity.

And yet my heart pangs for you
aches for nearness
How can it be, when you are already here?

Inside

The Art of Love-Making

"The Universe delights in creating." —Eckhart Tolle

Love-making is the art of creation stemming from our deepest selves. It matters not whether it's a poem, pottery, or new business idea—anything truly creative arises from our core, burning with the passion of Creation. On the universal level, the art of creation is the way the Universe may know itself, as it is constantly evidencing. On the microcosm level, creating is also the way we may know ourselves, learning both from the process of creating and from our creations themselves. And as our innate nature is Love, this is a form of Love giving rise to or 'making' love, i.e. the art of lovemaking. Here, I explore that art in the form of poetry.

A gentle poem
caresses me
as it flits by,
ready
to serve another.

Poetry is a reminder
of Who we are
and where we're from.

☙

I hear them as whispers
Sometimes on the air,
Sometimes in my heart

Begging to be born
        to be pinned to the page
        to be, at last, truly alive.

☙

Waiting for the poem that never comes.
Because I took too long,
        not snatching it from the air when it first appeared
I certainly felt compelled by its beauty
        but alas had no pen!
And now, feeling snubbed,
        it has moved on.

But here comes the next.

☙

I need the safety of my poems

    The captured ones
    The familiar ones

Which still whisper softly to me from the page
    where they've been pinned.

Reminding me gently of what's inside
    and that there is a safe joy
beyond the reach of the tumult
    surrounding me.

My familiars
    My respite
The bars of a jail I gladly pen
    for it represents freedom.

∽

Here I am,
    flowing onto a page.
Trying to untangle
    and pick apart
    the pieces
So I can better understand
    how to fit them together
    and give shape to purpose.

∽

Light is moving inside me,
thundering,
filtering in and out of every cell,
and every fiber,
A feeling of warmth and hope and joy
But without any escape

to this Love
that thunders
and echoes
within my walls,
It can only ease out
in the form
of poetry.

∾

100 words a minute pour from me
but none can compare to You
and our Love.
All shadows
crying out
trying to emulate
their Source
the One they Love.

∾

I see a poem
peeking its head timidly about the eaves
does it want to come and play?
I shall ask it
by picking up
my pen.

∾

Feeling all the feels…
as this smoky, swirling mass
inside me
rises up,
every emotion
every thought

occupying its own color,
each a spirit swirling
in the primordial juices of my Soul.
And just before your embrace
comes to snuff me out,
I want to feel all those feels
right out the end of this pen
and onto this sheet
of hope.

༄

A twinkle and pop
the poetry roils and fizzles inside
begging to come out and play
begging to be born

Pop
Spark
Splash

There she is
emanating from the ends of my fingers
a gentle twitch, flip, flex
of my pen
and there she is
lying naked and unashamed
in all her sensuous glory
on the page.

༄

Here it comes again
the gentle crest inside me
peaking
until

it crashes over the other side
ecstasy in motion
as my pen writhes
spraying out
another poem

∾

She seems breathy to me
after all that poetry writing
as though
she's been having sex
wrestling a naked foe
until submission is mutual,
all lying in a tangled heap
of love, sweat, tears
human hope
defined as
the endless dance
of poetry in motion.

Ah yes,
she has been writing poems.

∾

You Will Know

You will know
When there is a poem for you
For it will roll
from your very Inside
into the Outside
of the world

You will know

when there is a song for you
a task for you
a canvas for you
a book
a Soul to love and tend
a corner
a place
a fate

For they are rolling now
from your very Inside
being prepared for
your delight, your joy, your growth

You will know
if only
you sit
and you See.

༄

Instructions for Use

You've been given a power
you just don't know it
ordinary circumstances don't show it
because you're extraordinary

Can you see the glow, the electricity,
of your eyes, your hair, your fingertips?
Can you see the magic at your lips
as your heart swells open
giving birth to Love?

You are magic itself.

You have been born with something
inside you that you cannot see

To activate, you simply
have to press here
and here
and then

Just Be.

It is already yours,
always ready
for service.

∽

Sometimes I wish
that I could crack open my heart
and look deep inside,
scooping out all of the poems
and seeing
whether truly
the bottom is
endless

∽

I am scribbling with this pen
one verse per minute
flowing from my crevices
until there is no more.
See the wise being
trying to emerge
amid the noise
Hanuman's fate*

you are here to destroy
that which is
in place of that which Is
There is no more to be said.

* Hanuman is a figure from Hinduism renowned for his unwavering devotion to the Creator. Destruction here refers to the illusory elements of life.

Hunger for You

Humankind's unending search for God and for meaning is at the deepest level a search for ourselves, to know our innate nature. This is a fully pervasive soul hunger that pushes all the natural world to seek connection and completion. Perhaps nowhere is this more obvious than the act of love-making between two consensual bodies—a wild and savage calling humanity holds in its DNA. Sexual desire can lead to feelings of deep, fiery, unquenchable thirst and hunger. Even this discomfort holds its own beauty as we honor the physical form we dwell in. At its divine root, however, this hunger is the heart's longing to know itself.

Red light of passion
Fire, blood
it draws you on
seeking my warmth
in every corner
not realizing It
at your very Core

☙

Let me make Love to you
under the Light of the trees
The dawn's yearning
entering every pore
as you sit and swing
in Heaven.

☙

Let me make love to you
The ivy gently whispers to the tree
As she climbs the rough exterior
Leading her to naught
But Love

Let me make love to you
My lover whispers to me
As he spreads my thighs wide apart
Kissing gently where the lid has no eyes to see

Let me make love to you
The bee whispers to the flower
Let me make love to you
The dove calls to the wind

Let me make love
Let us make Love
Love is all there is

～

We create our own reality.

So here
    I am.

Wishing
    You
        to Me.

～

"I need to protect you," he says.

I don't want protection.

I want you to tear me asunder
          limb
              from
                   limb.
And I will enjoy every moment of your savage hunger,
As we remake me into wo-man.

～

If we were to kiss…

We would spend the next two days
wrapped in each other's scents and touch
arms and tongues and limbs
Entwined

Two becoming one
Over
      and over
            and over
The hot taste of you melted into my senses
Written into my warmth
Every fold yielding
to your infinite hunger and thirst
Coming
      again
           and again
To a new Beginning
   that is
      Wet
          and Explosive
                       and thoroughly explored.

IF we were to kiss…

∽

When we make love…

It will be glorious,
a dazzling of the senses
for our two human bodies.

But, our spirits are already entwined
in love-making.
Seeing each other, big and small,
Riding the summer winds,
Taking flight with the North-bound geese,
      honking their and our song
      with wild abandon,
Climbing volcanic mountains,
      their molten centers long cooled

        to life-filled waters, now misting the morning air,
Basking together in the sun-warmed grasses
      as our spirits roll together
      beneath the aqua sky,
      giggling in delight to just be
      Together
      One
      Entwined
           in love-making.

WHEN we make love…

∾

I don't like this
Balancing on a precipice
A knife's edge
    of feeling, savory drippy feeling
    tightly coiled inside my womanhood

The unquenchable need
might drive me mad
Un fuego* that can never be satisfied
no matter how many men
rush in bravely to fight the flames.

Perhaps, in place of the fire,
it would be better to have a blank sheet
of Nothingness.
But this promise of cooled limbs is, alas, not for me.

Spanish for "a fire"

∾

Unrequited Love

You did not say No,
you told me to Wait.

And so I did.

Until the flowers blossomed
        reaching their petals to the sun
        inviting bees and butterflies and all manner of
        sweetness drinkers
        seeding and spilling their future progeny to the soil
        and then withering and drying to a
        stiffened brown to feed the future.

Until the weather turned
        first crisp and cool, apples and pumpkins
        and all manner of spiced delight on my lips
        then cold and with teeth
        needing the warmth of fire and blanket and
        snoozy cat to comfort the bones and soul
        then blossoms again…
        then blazing heat…
        and again…
        and again…

Until the hills began to take new shape
        and the mountains crumbled
        and the seas quieted
        and the air grew thin
        and new things took limb and passed
        and took limb

Until the sun cooled and slept as stone

Until new stars were born and died and beyond

Until the Big Quiet.

And so I waited.

And so here I am, still

        Waiting.

            ∾

I see you there
every time
in my mind's eye
where I first created you

but a softer, more supple version
Warmer, gentler lips
        and encouraging, strong fingertips
Eyes that melt
        and bore through me

And here I meet you regularly
        as we escape together
to this place
        unbound by rules
                and time
Where all can be

Including Us.

            ∾

It hurts.
But that is what fuels us.

The tendrils of pain
        weaving through our being
Reminding us
        of sweetness
        which can only exist through contrast.

And so I come again and again
        to drink from this cup of fire
        though it never quenches my thirst.

        ☙

My love for you
threatens to break me open
set me free
Tearing me apart
        so that I can,
                at last,
        truly Become.

        ☙

Here I am, again, thinking of You
You of the golden feathers
flashing lights
announcing your arrival
into my heart

On a branch
you sit
preening
Only it is me
who suffers
to see your beauty
behold you
you, so close, yet so far out of reach

I extend my arms
My heart
seeking you
desperately
But you are not there.
Ephemeral.

Just as when I first Saw you.
Beauty.
Mesmerizing, just outside of
My reach.

∽

Stop thinking about Him,
     my mind bids my heart.
I cannot continue swimming in this ocean
     of lost love,
          every stroke an effort,
              my arms exhausted
                    as we lose ourselves
                        in Him.

I cannot stop thinking of Him,
     my heart replies.
But, He is the ocean,
     so rest awhile and let us float on our backs,
     gazing at the star-filled heavens,
     each burning point of light a testament
     to Him, Us, and what we represent.

We are Ocean, Sky, and all the Earth between,
     my love.
I cannot stop thinking of You,
     for We are One.

So let us rest in each other
        and Enjoy.

∽

I walk in your flame
and light my candle from it.
It will last me through today
as I face, with warmth, what's ahead.

But what I truly crave
is the eternal
Sitting in your light
with my many faces
warmed by the Sun.

It is a heart flame I am seeking
that glows with the light of one thousand suns
distributing your love
amongst us all.

∽

I love you
with every breath, every moment
A beacon of light
shining out from my heart
like a lighthouse
stopping ships from crashing on the rocks
But I am also the ship
wanting to crash ashore
just to walk with you again.

The sea calls to me
and releases me,

all in One.

∽

I feel so alive
with you inside me
I don't care for anything else
other than this Love
It encompasses all
and heals
with Light
and then we return
for more.
Boundless grace
and fullness
in each moment
Unadulterated by adornments
or falsities
as your Light burns away all deceit
Leaving only truth and Beauty.
I am here with you,
fashioning a new world
of possibilities
as we herald
the end, beginning
of what is now
into the next
and bring greater life, light, joy
for all to see.

∽

Life is beautiful
A tapestry of light and fire
the flames lashing higher and higher
as we reach for Beauty

And then through the blaze
a cooling relief
solely from Grace
to quench our thirst
as we drink
endlessly
of the Water of Life

You are my cooling Grace
from the fire in the pits of despair
caused by Separation
from the One I Love

∾

I fill my heart with Love,
and wait,
simmering,
waiting and hoping that what's next
is truly
already Here.
There is none other
than You.
No matter how I burn,
the answer returns
the same.
You
I
One We

∾

Your soft brown eyes
I look for them everywhere.
Silver pools of light,

reflecting our soul and infinite depths of love,
Wanting them and you to fill me endlessly.
A deep hunger of the heart.

And then,
I realize,
They were here all along,
in the mirror.

Feed the Children

The term "children" in a spiritual context represents the opportunity for all individuals to continue to awaken and grow into their deepest potential. Christ encouraged people to "change and become like little children" (Matt 18:3) to access this state of divine innocence. We are the many-faceted aspects of divine manifestation knowing itself and growing through a journey of self-discovery. This state of child-like innocence and curiosity is what allows us to notice the abundance surrounding us in each moment, thereby making it truly accessible to us as the gift it is. The accompanying spirit of acceptance and allowance enables each of us to walk in what is "special" about ourselves and each other, entering a unified state of Oneness with our earthly family. Turning from noise, distraction, and loneliness, we discover instead the wisdom and wealth within. This then elevates each aspect of the world around us, yielding infinite opportunities for our mutual transformation and delight. We are fed and feasting, nourished on the most fulfilling level imaginable. This in turn enables us to support others in our earthly family to become fed and sated.

How beautiful
the many forms of me
quaking, quivering
with eager anticipation
knowing yet not Knowing
how it is to come

☙

Father's Gifts

Sometimes my Father likes to give me gifts
The unexpected beckoning of a poem
The round, dew-glittering shape of a fruit
A painting that births itself on my canvas
A bird adorned in bright red or blue
gazing in at my breakfast window

Sometimes He gives me gifts
but only when I open up my eyes

Sometimes He gives me gifts
but only because I'm Special

like each and every one of You,
His Sons and Daughters,
All Special
and all here together
in Magnificence.

☙

Let them come
let them come
and I will show them Your Love

how it drips from the eaves
for all children to receive
heads tilted back
eyes glittering
joy and mischief in the air
eagerness in every muscle
as they receive
your benediction.

∾

On Prayer

Your red lips
press against the glass
asking for another kiss.
But now is not the time
for love-making.
It is time for the stew
to be poured
into each bowl
that all the children
may be fed.

∾

Gentle child, awaken.

You are asked to give birth
to awaken each day ready to serve
ready to receive whatever blessing
whatever mystery arises
using that leavening
to bake bread.

A culture follows you

and it is delicious in its warmth.

～

A gentle power
roars inside me
waiting to make her debut.

She knows why she's come,
She knows why she's here,
and she's waiting to demonstrate to you:

You are here
You are here
in your gentle power too.

～

The Self-less Self-ishness

It is the reason I serve
Why I cannot turn
from an empty bowl
without filling it with rice
Why I cannot turn
from a child
until I whisper something nice
Why I cannot close
my eyes
or my wallet
when I see your fear
your pain

I cannot do anything
but serve Me,
the many forms of Me,

for service is Love
is Truth
is Purpose
is Wisdom
is the very Being of Everything.

And I am here,
awake and alive,
serving You
And You, I.

∽

The Stillness between us is too much
and so we reach for more
pulling it around us
nestling in
to share
with the ones we love.
The World.

∽

The nameless Glory of You
Every inch perfection
Infinity beckons
Her children home

∽

Beat the drum of my heart
Beat it for Me
beat it loudly
Beat the drum of my heart
it is Here for You
it sways wildly in the wind

it pounds with resonance
at your fingertips

My drum
My heart
is with you
always
The crying, starving baby
The anguished, empty soul
The sounds of traffic
filling our minds
but never our hearts

Beat the drum of my heart
for it is your drum
One Drum
beating
waiting
for infinity
that never comes
for it's already Here.

Feel the Drum.

∾

We'll speak next at the break

Light breaks
Dawn
Your heart breaks
Dawn
See with your own eyes
Shape with your own hands

The table is filled with items to feast

But only you wait there
Why not dig in
Sate your hunger and your tears

I see you lurking at the garden door
Shy to enter
Too aroused to leave
Come in
Come in and feast

∾

I cannot hold the world on my shoulders
    for they are not broad enough
        to carry the pains, sorrows, joys, surprises
    of each life daring to be

But

I can carry the world in my heart
    its infinite depth a nest that the world
    can be settled into
    nestled and held, in love,
    the warm breath of hope and acceptance and patience
    a whisper, saying always,

    I love you.

∾

Loneliness is like shouting into the void
    See me! Hear me! Love me!
    and yet it persists
This heavy blanket, weighing us down
This empty feeling, coiling its way around our insides
    squeezing our hearts and spirits

       relentlessly shooting arrows into our minds

So pervasive, so invasive.
How can so many people, standing all together,
       feel so lonely?

Here I am, with you,
       seeing you, hearing you, loving you.

So you can see, hear, love yourself.

∾

Your eyes
I saw them yesterday
on the man in the streets
His lips were rippled in pain
his voice full of anguish
for the family he is seeking
But his eyes
were deep pools
of infinite light
"Mírame"* I said
and as he looked up,
I saw myself
and I saw
the infinite love
that is you
that is us.

One sandwich,
one walk,
one action item later,
and he was gone.
His body no longer
at the train station,

his spirit returned to you,
my heart returned to me.

* Spanish for "look at me"

∞

Thread the needle
and sew a tapestry
of light and color
with your song
you shall fill the world

Do not wait
until you hear what awaits you
but act with compassion
and the steady light
of flow.

∞

The game

It is played
first with one
then with two
The glue is
togetherness.
How do you encompass it?
You wait
and then
you Go.
Go forth and multiply
go forth and Be.

∽

Circle

You surround me
a circle of community
a beacon of Light
and reminder of what's to come.

Community,
a healing that cannot be broken,
because it emanates
from the highest frequency of who we are
Reminding us
as we look around
that we are all Here
all Together
all fully perfect in the Light.

Take my hand, friend,
and let's circle
and dance
in the Light.

∽

Playing Hide n Seek

Everywhere I go
they are looking for Me

My children seek
but they do not find

How to find the One
who is so cleverly

already hidden in plain sight
in front of you
Everywhere

A Lovely World

When we see the world with fresh eyes, its inherent loveliness steps forward, a mirror to our own being. Each moment is then filled with awe as we delight in what we discover about ourselves and the abundance of the Universe. Daily miracles occur both in the ordinary being transformed into the extraordinary, and in our own increasing encounters with our deepest mystical self. It is a re-cognition that our Creator has left so many marks of Love in this world and in our own hearts, if we will only slow enough to notice them. In embracing this Deep Truth, we are given a beautiful gift—access to co-create the world itself. This starts first in our imagination and then moves from that place of potential into the fabric of reality.

She's pregnant again.
The Day is pregnant with potential.

Each moment starting with
Hope, possibility, creativity
A whisper of what could be
Bridging, reaching out, to hold the hand of what is

If you listen carefully,
You will see.

If you look carefully,
You will hear.

The colorful note on the air,
Beckoning You.

To Birth.

∽

We shall see
when we open up
to the blue sky
the beauty of the day
the flowering of a blossom
the bird, a red cardinal, chirping on a spring branch

It is here
the kingdom, the promised heaven
and it does not need to be sought
only Seen.

And the more eyes that See,
the closer It gets.

∽

Silence awaits

The forest is full of trees
Listening
For what's to come
and What Is

∽

Destiny's Wing

She holds me, cradled, under her wings
The span greater than time
              than space
              than my own limited dreams
And when she flies
        she takes me with her
        soaring over the seas, the tundras,
        past anything I could have held in imagination

and into
        My Self.

∽

Hello my beauty
I sit here quietly at the window
Wondering
if you can see me, hear me,
reach out and touch me.
I have never left
and I am here to help
I see you in your journey
highs & lows

sweetness & sorrow
Dichotomies and yet there are none.
I see you.

∽

God is in Everything
in every minute
    every morsel
    every cell
    every vibration

The sound of a mother crying
as her baby takes its first steps

The feel of the carpet
squishing between the toes
as the baby gurgles with delight

The gurgle of the baby,
its high-pitched shriek of joy,
Joy of discovery
as it crosses the room
and irritates the snoozing cat

The twitching ears of the annoyed cat
that pick up the sound vibrations
and lay back a few millimeters,
Reminding
that not everyone
wants to hear
God's shriek of joy
at 4 in the morning.

∽

How well do you have to know something
to teach it?
Does this Song from my Heart count?
It is thousands of years old
and yet
I am still learning
to recognize its notes.

∽

Same Shadow

Hamsayeh*
she whispers
My Persian self
telling me the thousand-year truth
that we are all the same
all one
from our source
our deepest depth
our shadowy selves
our tippy toes to our twinkling teeth
otherwise
how could it be
that we have the
Same Shadow

* Persian for "neighbor" but more literally may be interpreted as shadows occurring together or "same shadow"

∽

There is work to do

Father and Mother are coming this morning

Nathaniel too
and that annoying cocker spaniel!

We must clear the dishes from last night's supper
Sweep the hearth
Lay the ironed cloths
Bring in fresh milk and honey
The risen bread needs a bake
The Earth needs continue its orbit
The planets need align around the Sun
Gravitational forces
gaseous energies
matter and the vacuum of space
all in check
Creation needs to be ongoingly preserved,
billions of births and deaths to attend to today
Oh!
And the butter
I forgot the butter needs a fresh churning.
Mother only likes fresh butter.

Okay,
you take those,
and I'll take these,
and together we'll get it all done in time.

∞

The smile of your hand
as you caress me,
a warm spot of sunshine.
Even if I can't see,
I can feel.
And your presence wraps itself around me
like a warm blanket.
Forever yours,

forever here,
I wait.

I see you
waiting here
to speak to me.
But I have nothing to say.
Go
Listen to the sound of the wind.

༄

The sunlight kisses the tears from my lids
As she drapes herself around my face
Warming me, preparing me,
For His touch.

༄

Hope, on a whispered wing,
      visits me.
My only companion
      in the storm
      of my mind.
Bidding me,
      Wait for it,
      wait.
      wait.
            for it is coming,
And It is Beautiful.

༄

"In two days it will be tomorrow," he said
as he handed me a glass of wine.

"Rumi," I laughed, "this is your glass.
Please don't forget to pour yourself one too."

∾

Grow and be abundant
reach for the stars
as you did last night
when you saw Me twinkling
I am a light at the gallows
I am the storm in the furnace
I enter where No One sees
and I leave without leaving.
Listen carefully and you will hear
the song I have written on your heart
Telling you
Calling you
to Wisdom.

Be the free form
of day
Be the angel of night
You do not sleep
but you whisper always
quietly
then as a Roar.

Tomorrow is Here.

∾

We remake ourselves every day
Born again
into a world of our own design
What we see
        See

    SEE
or, think we do,
builds that world
      block by block.

But.

We are convinced
it is the other way around.

And that the World happens to us.
Creating us
Impacting us
Us.
with little choice in the matter.

See.
Create.
The loom awaits,
   with bated breath.

∾

The Canvas
It starts blank,
beckoning our imaginations to color.
To pick the color that will best
represent
our hopes, our humanity,
The color of the eagle soaring
with a cry over the mountains,
The color of our grandmother and mother
grinding nutrients in a mortar with pestle,
The color of grass
wild and swaying in the breeze,
The color of sun as it shines

through, not on, the leaves,
The color of the geese and ducks
as they bathe with glee in the frozen waters,
The color of atoms and stardust,
The color of all of us,
Humans, as One.

And as we pick out our colors
and put brush to canvas,
we see the edges expanding
and rediscover the Canvas itself,
with new eyes.

∾

A light in the dark
A promise of what's to come
Hope's edge twinkling with sparks
as her blade slashes through the old
and brings forth birth and new life

∾

I saw you today
in the sparks on the ground
as the snow plow flinted with the concrete
bursts of light in the night
just like the light tunnel
of the flowing snow flakes
dancing in my car beam lights.
Every speck of light
every whisper of song
in this world
is You.
The caress of a woman to her baby
or between two lovers.

The song of a bird
waking to the dawn.
The hope of a team
whether in a hospital operating room
or on a field where dreams are born.
Every moment
every love song
every breath
is You.
And I have not the pretty words
to bring forth
for this occasion
we call The Present.

[Silence is You.]

༄

The morning light
splashes so beautifully across the page
And so do You
across my heart
unfettered from a thousand years
of solitude
Love
is all I seek and all that I am.
Here with you
in this moment.

༄

Every moment is a Song.

If you sit and listen carefully
You will hear the notes on the air

and in your Heart
for they are One.

But if you stayed open this long
                    this fully
                        all the time,
You would Melt, for the Beauty of the World
    and for not Knowing Her sooner.

Nature Speaks

"And then my heart with pleasure fills, and dances with the daffodils."
—Wordsworth

Nowhere else is the interconnectedness and Oneness of all of Life more apparent than in the arms of Mother Nature. Both creative and destructive forces are in harmony within her, each acting as one side of the coin within universal evolution and growth. She offers a feast for the senses, calling us to awaken. She serves as one of our greatest teachers, ever present to the willing, eager student. Full of both quiet and roaring metaphors, she beckons us back to our Selves. An interactive, tantalizing game awaits in each moment with her as we throb with the pulse of Life.

The Sun
the Earth, the air, the very Sky
beckons you
to
Completion.

∽

The soft earth
she calls to me
a hallowed blanket
of wet and warm and wild.

She asks me,
Why aren't you here?
Basking, healing, squishing
your toes into my inviting embrace…

I reply…
I don't know.
Come to think of it,
I have no excuse.
No deadlines, no redlines,
no computer, no phone,
nothing can keep me away from you.
That's why I try, and I cry,
and I keep coming back
for more.
Dripping my sorrows
dipping my toes
into your warm, earthy soil.
Watching the robins, the butterflies
flutter by.
Each of us a reminder
of who we all truly are
Together.

❧

The smell of your sweet pollen
The touch of your warm Spring breeze
The call of your titillating birds
The sight of you in every sun-kissed leaf
If this isn't Love,
I don't know what I am tasting.

❧

Water

I ask for what I cannot see
and what comes to me is
Water

Sparkling, twinkling
life-giving
thirst-inducing
so much
Water

coating the earth
my cells
my Heart
my deepest Being
Water

Water connects us
in the ocean
we call Home.

The Nest

You sit there
angrily warbling
wondering why I won't leave
until you notice
I am your warble
tickling the Love
right up from your throat.
Hello.

Do you know me, blue jay?
For you and I are one
Playing sleeping games
and seeing who wakes first.
I think I have the advantage
as I already Love You.

Walk with me
and you will See
the Source of this Joy
sitting
gently
on my finger.
Hello.

∽

Dancing gnats

They buzz and buzz around me
Do you see?
If I were not so busy,
being annoyed,
I might notice them
calling me
to myself.

∽

Listen, they sigh,
just listen.
The trees beckon me
to earth
to birth
to you
to myself.

∽

Hello, wild mangy dog,
who is it I see in your eyes?
It is the whippoorwill
and its haunting call
It is the cypress
and its gracious curves
A thousand hurricanes, tornados, volcanos
All lead me to you.

∾

She bends her slender waist
and throws her arms up
in silent reverence
And then he swings by
Kissing her arms, her thighs,
her earth shattering.
Such idolatry
cannot be tolerated
except for the One
as the wind
makes love
to the trees.

She bends her very boughs to the earth
Her every leaf
Whispering
Take me, take me
as he passes.

Love has no bounds
even less so
when your Lord is the earth.

∾

The Nut.

She picked it up, examined it in her hands,
Shiny, smooth, brown
So beautiful.
Her eyes shone with desire.

The outer layer loosened,
And she saw inside a fibrous spindly bundle,

Surprising interconnected networks,
Quirky fun in how they supported the center,
Releasing an intoxicating sweet chocolate smell.
Her mouth watered with delight.

She whispered softly to it,
And the center revealed itself.

Opening,
She saw the stars sparkling,
Spinning galaxies,
Birds of every color, shape, size,
Water whispering through streams, roaring through falls,
Sunlight on a patch of inviting grass,
The earth forming, reforming, shaping itself over millennia.

Her soul smiled. And was sated.

∽

I touch my hand to your walls
Smooth enamel, ivory, with small
cracks pulsing through,
Each a memory of a stress
you've endured.

Stepping into your curved corridors,
I feel the grit of sand crunching
under my heel

Round and round your walls
continue to curve.
A mystery at the center,
and only a vacuous echo
of ocean sounds to encourage me on.

I put you down, Seashell, with some difficulty
extracting myself from my whimsical stroll.

～

What gives the leaves of the trees
        this wanton daring
to shimmer and dance
        and shake their hips and arms
in the glory of the wind
        while paying homage to the Sun
        with their glimmering faces

What are they whispering in glee
    as She and He whip by them, on them, through them

Only the blades of grass
will hint at the answer
As they too beam up at me,
reflecting Her light
        each one a small sun unto herself.

～

I Love her instantly.

The graceful curve of her neck
Her haunting black-rimmed eyes
The swoop of midnight mane gracing her head
Her feathery dress as she walks along the water's edge,
shimmering sometimes blue, sometimes grey, sometimes white
in the light of the early morning sun.

As I peer through the trees by the pond,
I try to get a closer look at her,
my only misstep the snap of a twig under foot,

disturbing the morning quiet.

Without a glance in my direction
She takes off
Soaring
My Great Blue Heron
Leaving me
A jilted Lover

∽

A cold winter day
It feels sad for the branches are bare
        the buds dead
        the dew frosted
        the birds huddled down and quiet
        the sun too far away
        to make a difference

And yet something inside me rebels
                      and yells

Come and see
        how under the surface
        the roots gather energy,
        readying themselves for the next boisterous spring
Come and see
        how the ants and people still mill about
        storing and saving
        preparing to celebrate
        preparing for rest
        encouraging each other in this season of joint cheer
Come and see
        how the snow flutters so beautifully
        as it dances down to kiss the earth
        how graceful footprints of plant and meat eater

                    write stories in the white blanket of the earth
Come and see
Sit quietly with me
And See.

∾

The soul dance in winter

So fragrant is the spring
but it cannot touch
the spirit of the soul dance in winter
The clumps of snow
drizzle in the sky
ever downward softly
I see them but feel them also
in my spirit
and so I get up too
and I dance to the music
of water
that connects us all
I dance and I sway
I swirl and I twirl
every limb a living melody
in harmony with life.

∾

The song of the birds
adds a vibrant color
to the tapestry of life,
weaving its way into our veins
Life blood
coursing
through each artery
seeking to find

the Center
the Heart
where we can rest
in Love

∽

We start our day
Euphoric
with potential
each breath of our lungs, our trees,
united in the dance of what's to come

We don't need prettied words
to confess Our Love.

Only this.

Look out the window
See the trees
swaying in their splendor
Relax your muscles, your tension,
and enter
the Beloved's world.

We shall know each other again.
Come.

∽

A soft cloud
sits in the stillness of blue,
surrounded by emptiness.
It does not wonder
where it is,
held up instead

by belief
by hope
for what Is and can be.

∽

I look at the light energy
outside
it flows through me
and I am reborn

A baby robin sits in its nest
naked and waiting
In comes mama
with a worm
a feathery red breast
a promise of warmth, care, comfort

I hold the reins
and await
your glory
manifest here
where we are all waiting
your promise
of warmth, care, comfort

∽

A spring blade
she sways in the wind
open to what comes
living as if
it's already Here.

∽

The only true sound
is that of the footsteps
walking in the woods
Guiding us back to ourselves

~

The natural morning light
so soft and still, I sit
Here I can see
what is and can be
But, alas, I also hearken
to the sound
of my own beating heart
returning to the source
of all that is.
Why am I Here?
To Be.
The birds sing in delight
at my discovery
in the morning light.
Poems do not end
♪♫♪♫♪

~

She kisses me
The day gently kisses me good morning
Shedding her twilight gown
for one bathed in pale rosy hues
of pink, orange,
hemmed in pale blue.

She wants me to Open my eyes
and See

how much potential there is between us
and how she longs to hold me
each day
as we try together
for a beautiful tomorrow.

Birth is not a difficult process,
but completely natural when we let go,
For all of creation wants to line up
to support us.

The sky is but one palette
for the artist to draw upon.

I Am

"The tao that can be told, is not the eternal Tao."—Tao Te Ching

No words, sounds, images can capture the infinite. There are things which surpass conceptual thought, yet the poet, the artist endlessly seeks to express in a myriad of ways unity with the divine state. This infinite state is the truest state of humankind. There is nothing we need do or become to access and deserve it. It is our incredulity at the benevolence of this miraculous gift that keeps us from it. It is already Here, but requires a release of all we thought we knew. Spiritual texts refer to transcending duality to realize unity nature, and ultimately merging back into infinite potential, the Stillness from which the Universe arose.

Nowhere to be but here

I am not a poet
I am not a person
I am no one
and yet

I see you

and that makes me

You.

∾

What is in motion?
Everything.
But
at the deepest level
Not I,
held in stillness.

∾

Shhhh… Can you hear the Stillness?
It is always there
beckoning
singing softly our name
I Am
I Am Here.
Always and Now.

No One can hear.
I Am No One.

∾

My heart aches with pleasure
it takes my breath away
as I Breathe into Life
Me.

∾

Here, I am Here,
and I belong to no man or woman
but All
I am the wind that sweeps thru the trees
I am the gardener on his knees
picking the ripest strawberries
and holding them to the eager lips
of his grandchild.
I am the storm in the sky
that whips around the corners
of skyscrapers
howling, bowing to No One.
I am you and me
as we sit together and picnic
a knowing love
growing
in our eyes.
I am the soles of your feet
the souls of your innermost heart
Your Heart
Your Head
Your Body.
I am You
Darling
and you
are
Infinite.

∾

You are my Child
the gentle caress of the warm breeze
stirs in you
an aching
an awakening
a wonder
as you realize you are Me.
We. As the world was made.

༄

I am Here

She who waits
waits eagerly
with patience
for what's to come
The arriving
is Here

༄

This is my love song
You ache to see me
Searching me out everywhere
The trees, the sky, the mountains
under rocks, in birds' nests,
in others' eyes
And the Truth is
I am right here
Looking at you
in the mirror

You and I
One
All One

❧

I feel you coursing
through my every bone
my marrow
hums with the delight of you.
A message of beauty
written into my very core
saying
I am coming. I am Here.

❧

I am Enough

I am enough to dance the heavens
my robe skimming star surfaces behind me.
I am enough to deserve Your Love
its infinite Grace given simply because I exist.
I am enough to be with you
holding your hand in the infancy
of my adulthood, my rebirth.
I am enough
I am enough
because you created me So
So it will Be
So it Is.

Thank you.

❧

When I see you
I unearth a beauty
beyond measure
In each moment
beckoning me to
myself.

∽

You do not see your own beauty
And so you try to ascribe it to me
The One who watches.

∽

I am nothing and no one
and yet
I see
everything
in this moment
with You.
Held by your silence
in Beauty.

∽

To hear my Father's Voice
is a beautiful thing
especially
when it emerges
from
Me.

∽

Because it is The Way

I am Here
and can Be nowhere and no one else

～

What is the question?
Who are you?

To Be
is all there is
The Is-ness is Here
and awaits your command.

I do not fret
for sight of you.
I do not seek
what is already Here.

I Am.

～

The Journey

The journey is not an easy one,
filled with corpses
of what we held dear
our hopes, our fears,
our knowing of who we are
replaced by
our Knowing of Who We Are
who I Am

It is not an easy journey
but it is a blessed one
filled with Knowing Joy

knowing comfort,
not of the warm blanket or cup of tea,
but of the Soul
of the great reuniting
with the One who is
the Creator
of all
including
little us.

So grand are we in our mystery.

www.ingramcontent.com/pod-product-compliance
Lightning Source LLC
Chambersburg PA
CBHW071721090426
42738CB00009B/1840